99 1/p 2108

Carbon

and the Group 4 Elements

THE PERIODIC TABLE

Nigel Saunders

Heinemann LIBRARY

www.heinemann.co.uk/library

Visit our website to find out more information about Heinemann Library books.

To order:
☎ Phone 44 (0) 1865 888066
📄 Send a fax to 44 (0) 1865 314091
💻 Visit the Heinemann Bookshop at www.heinemann.co.uk/library to browse our catalogue and order online.

First published in Great Britain by Heinemann Library, Halley Court, Jordan Hill, Oxford OX2 8EJ, part of Harcourt Education.
Heinemann is a registered trademark of Harcourt Education Ltd.

Editorial: Sarah Eason and Kathy Peltan
Design: David Poole and Tinstar Design Limited (www.tinstar.co.uk)
Illustrations: Geoff Ward and Paul Fellows
Picture Research: Rosie Garai
Production: Viv Hichens
Originated by Blenheim Colour Ltd
Printed and bound in China by South China.

ISBN 0 431 16982 9
07 06 05 04 03
10 9 8 7 6 5 4 3 2 1

British Library Cataloguing in Publication Data
Saunders, Nigel
    Carbon and the group 4 elements.
    – (The periodic table)
    546.6'8
A full catalogue record for this book is available from the British Library.

Acknowledgements
The publishers would like to thank the following for permission to reproduce photographs:
Corbis pp10 (Stuart Westmorland), 11 (Vanni Archive), 15 (Rick Gayle), 19 (Lee Snider), 40 (Adam Woolfitt), 48 (Adam Woolfitt), 50 (Bob Krist), 52 (Owen Franken); Getty Images p4 (Robin Smith [Stone]); Oxford Scientific Films p29 (Adam Jones); Science Photo Library pp8 (Peter Menzel), 9 (Charles Falco), 12, 13 (Martin Bond), 17 (Andrew McClenaghan), 21 (Kaj R. Svensson), 22 (Martin Bond), 26 (Matt Meadows), 30 (Astrid & Hans Frieder Michler), 37 (Kazuyoshi Nomachi), 38 (B. Kramer/Custom Medical Stock Photo), 43 (David Taylor), 44 (Novosti), 47, 49 (Arnold Fisher), 54/5 (Oscar Burriel), 57 (Geoff Tompkinson); Trevor Clifford pp25, 32.

Cover photograph of diamonds reproduced with permission of Getty Images.

The author would like to thank Angela, Kathryn, David and Jean for all their help and support.

The publishers would like to thank Alexandra Clayton for her assistance in the preparation of this book.

Contents

Words appearing in bold, **like this**, are explained in the Glossary

CHAPTER 1

Elements and atomic structure

Have you ever wondered how many different substances there are in the world? If you look around, you'll see metals, plastics, water and lots of other solids and liquids. Although you can't see the gases in the air, you know they are there. There are many other gases too. Just how many different substances are there? Incredibly, over 19 million different substances have been discovered, named and catalogued. Around 4000 substances are added to the list each day, yet all of these substances are made from just a few simple building blocks called **elements**.

Elements

There are about 92 naturally occurring elements and a few artificial ones, including element number 114 in group 4. Elements are materials that cannot be broken down into simpler substances using chemical **reactions**. About three-quarters of the elements are metals, such as tin and lead, and most of the rest are non-metals, such as carbon and oxygen. Some elements, like germanium and silicon, are called metalloids because they have some of the properties of metals and some of the properties of non-metals.

This thrilling rollercoaster and its riders are made from some of the millions of chemicals in the world. ▶

Compounds

Elements can join together in chemical reactions to make **compounds**. For example, lead and oxygen react together to make lead oxide, and carbon and oxygen react together to make carbon dioxide. This means that nearly all of the millions of different substances in the world are compounds, made up of two or more elements chemically joined together.

Atoms

Every substance is made up of tiny particles called **atoms**. An element is made up of just one type of atom, and a compound is made up of two or more types of atom joined together. Atoms are far too small to see, even with a light microscope. If you could line up carbon atoms side by side along a fifteen-centimetre ruler, you would need a billion of them!

Atoms themselves are made up of even tinier particles called **protons**, **neutrons** and **electrons**. At the centre of each atom there is a **nucleus** made up of protons and neutrons. The electrons are arranged in different energy levels, or shells, around the nucleus. Most of an atom is actually empty space – if an atom were blown up to the same size as an Olympic running track, its nucleus would be about the size of a pea! The electrons, and how they are arranged, are responsible for the ways in which each element can react.

Elements and groups

Different elements react with other substances in different ways. When chemists first began to study chemical reactions this made it difficult for them to make sense of the reactions they observed. In 1869, a Russian chemist called Dimitri Mendeleev put each element into one of eight groups in a table. Each group contained elements with similar chemical properties. This made it much easier for chemists to work out what to expect when they reacted elements with each other. You can find the modern equivalent, the **periodic table**, on the next page.

The periodic table, group 4 and carbon

Chemists built on Mendeleev's work and eventually produced the modern **periodic table**, shown below. Each row in the table is called a **period**. The elements in a period are arranged in order of increasing **atomic number** (the atomic number is the number of **protons** in the **nucleus**). Each column in the table is called a **group**. The **elements** in each group have similar chemical properties to each other. For example, the elements in group 1 are very reactive, soft metals, and the elements in group 0 are very unreactive gases. It is called the periodic table because these different chemical properties occur regularly, or periodically. The elements in each group also have the same number of electrons in their outer shell. The elements in group 4 all have four electrons in their outer shell.

▼ *This is the periodic table of the elements; all the metals are on the left, and all the non-metals are on the right. Group 4 contains carbon which is a non-metal, two metalloids (silicon and germanium) and three metals (tin, lead and ununquadium).*

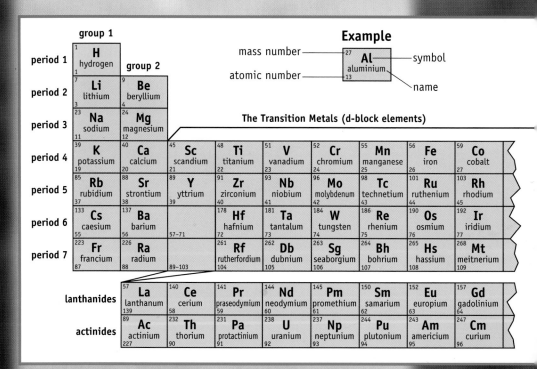

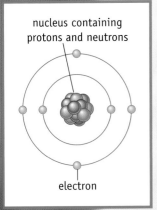

nucleus containing
protons and neutrons

electron

◀ *A model of an atom of carbon. Every element has a
different number of protons (atomic number). A carbon
atom contains six protons and six neutrons. Its electrons
are arranged in two shells around the nucleus.*

As you go down each group, the chemical properties
of the elements change gradually. Carbon, at the top
of group 4, is a non-metal with a high melting point.
Silicon and germanium, in the middle of the group, are
metalloids, while tin and lead at the bottom are metals
with low melting points. There is also an artificial
element in group 4, below lead. Very few **atoms** of
this element have been made, which is temporarily called
ununquadium (pronounced 'yoon-oon-kwad-ium'). We do not
know very much about it because its atoms give off radiation
and break down to form other elements within seconds of being
made. However, chemists are certain that it is a metal because
the elements immediately above it in group 4 are both metals.

Group 4 and carbon
In this book, you are going to find out all about carbon and
the other elements in group 4, the **compounds** they make,
and many of their uses.

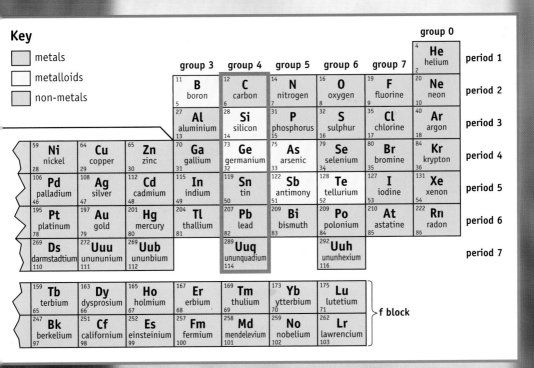

Key

- metals
- metalloids
- non-metals

group 0

| | group 3 | group 4 | group 5 | group 6 | group 7 | 4 **He** helium 2 | period 1 |

| 11 **B** boron 5 | 12 **C** carbon 6 | 14 **N** nitrogen 7 | 16 **O** oxygen 8 | 19 **F** fluorine 9 | 20 **Ne** neon 10 | period 2 |

| 27 **Al** aluminium 13 | 28 **Si** silicon 14 | 31 **P** phosphorus 15 | 32 **S** sulphur 16 | 35 **Cl** chlorine 17 | 40 **Ar** argon 18 | period 3 |

| 59 **Ni** nickel 28 | 64 **Cu** copper 29 | 65 **Zn** zinc 30 | 70 **Ga** gallium 31 | 73 **Ge** germanium 32 | 75 **As** arsenic 33 | 79 **Se** selenium 34 | 80 **Br** bromine 35 | 84 **Kr** krypton 36 | period 4 |

| 106 **Pd** palladium 46 | 108 **Ag** silver 47 | 112 **Cd** cadmium 48 | 115 **In** indium 49 | 119 **Sn** tin 50 | 122 **Sb** antimony 51 | 128 **Te** tellurium 52 | 127 **I** iodine 53 | 131 **Xe** xenon 54 | period 5 |

| 195 **Pt** platinum 78 | 197 **Au** gold 79 | 201 **Hg** mercury 80 | 204 **Tl** thallium 81 | 207 **Pb** lead 82 | 209 **Bi** bismuth 83 | 209 **Po** polonium 84 | 210 **At** astatine 85 | 222 **Rn** radon 86 | period 6 |

| 269 **Ds** darmstadtium 110 | 272 **Uuu** unununium 111 | 269 **Uub** ununbium 112 | | 289 **Uuq** ununquadium 114 | | 292 **Uuh** ununhexium 116 | | | period 7 |

| 159 **Tb** terbium 65 | 163 **Dy** dysprosium 66 | 165 **Ho** holmium 67 | 167 **Er** erbium 68 | 169 **Tm** thulium 69 | 173 **Yb** ytterbium 70 | 175 **Lu** lutetium 71 | > f block |
| 247 **Bk** berkelium 97 | 251 **Cf** californium 98 | 252 **Es** einsteinium 99 | 257 **Fm** fermium 100 | 258 **Md** mendelevium 101 | 259 **No** nobelium 102 | 262 **Lr** lawrencium 103 | |

Elements of group 4

There are six **elements** in group 4: carbon, silicon, germanium, tin, lead and ununquadium. They are all solids at room temperature. Carbon is a non-metal whereas tin, lead and ununquadium are metals. Silicon and germanium are metalloids, which means that their properties are between those of metals and non-metals.

12	C carbon	**carbon**
6		symbol: C • atomic number: 6 • non-metal

Coal, charcoal and soot are almost pure carbon, so it is likely that people have known about carbon for thousands of years. The name carbon comes from the Latin word meaning charcoal. However, carbon was not clearly recognized as an element until the 18th century.

What does it look like? There are different forms of carbon that look very different from each other. These different forms are called **allotropes** of carbon. Graphite and diamond are the best-known allotropes of carbon. Graphite is the shiny black solid used in pencil 'lead', and diamond is the clear, colourless solid often seen in jewellery. These allotropes exist because of the different ways carbon **atoms** can join together. Carbon also exists as **amorphous** carbon (found in soot), as microscopic hollow tubes called nanotubes, and as spherical molecules called fullerenes.

Where is it found? Carbon can form a vast number of compounds and it is found almost everywhere on Earth. Carbon dioxide makes up 0.035 per cent of the atmosphere and it is dissolved in rivers, lakes and seas. Many minerals and rocks contain carbon **compounds**. Natural gas and crude oil contain compounds of hydrogen and carbon called **hydrocarbons**. Chains and rings of carbon

Crude oil gushing out of an oil well damaged by the Iraqis during the invasion of Kuwait. Oil contains a complex mixture of many different carbon compounds.

atoms are the vital component in the complex molecules of life itself, and all living things contain carbon. There is a lot of carbon in your body – over 20 per cent of your mass is due to carbon!

28	**Si** silicon	**silicon**
14		*symbol: Si • atomic number: 14 • metalloid*

The Swedish chemist Jöns Berzelius, who introduced many of the chemical symbols we use today, discovered silicon in 1823.

What does it look like? There are two allotropes of silicon: a dark red-brown powder called amorphous silicon, and a shiny grey-black solid called crystalline silicon.

Where is it found? Silicon is the second most abundant element in the Earth's crust, but it is usually found combined with the most abundant element, oxygen, in various silicon dioxides. Sand is the best-known silicon dioxide, and there are many others, such as quartz and flint. The name silicon comes from the Latin word for flint. **Minerals** such as granite and asbestos also contain silicon, and tiny living things called diatoms build their cell walls using silicon compounds.

What are its main uses? Silicon and its compounds are extremely useful to us. Silicon with tiny amounts of other elements is an important **semi-conductor** material, used widely in electronic devices. Silicon compounds are used in glass, concrete, brick, pottery and silicone sealants.

▼ *This computer microchip contains very pure crystalline silicon containing tiny amounts of other elements.*

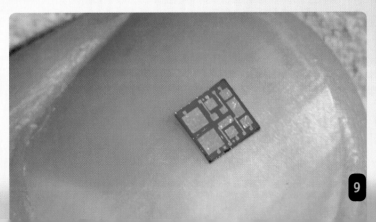

More elements of group 4

73	
Ge	
germanium	
32	

germanium
symbol: Ge • atomic number: 32 • metalloid

Clemens Winkler, a German chemist, discovered germanium in 1886. The name germanium comes from the Latin word for Germany.

What does it look like and where is it found? Germanium is a **brittle** grey-white crystalline solid found in a number of **minerals**. These include argyrodite (from which it was first isolated) and germanite, which contains 8 per cent germanium.

What are its main uses? Germanium is an important **semi-conductor** material used in all sorts of electronic devices. Telephone and cable television networks use optical fibres made from glass containing germanium to carry their signals. Germanium is also used in fluorescent lights and in high-quality lenses for microscopes and cameras.

119	
Sn	
tin	
50	

tin
symbol: Sn • atomic number: 50 • metal

Tin is an Anglo-Saxon word, but the symbol comes from the Latin word for tin (*stannum*).

What does it look like and where is it found? Tin metal cannot be found in its native form as a free **element**, but it has been known for thousands of years. As bronze is an **alloy** of tin and copper, it is clear that tin has been in use, at least, since the Bronze Age (4000 years ago). Casserite, tin oxide, is the most important tin ore.

When barnacles and other sea creatures live on the hulls of ships, the ships use more fuel. Paints containing tin compounds stop these creatures growing. But on sunken wrecks they can grow without hindrance.

There are two **allotropes** of tin, which can be converted into each other by heating or cooling. Ordinary tin is a **malleable** (easily worked) silvery-white solid. When this is cooled below 13.2 °C, it slowly changes into a brittle grey solid that turns back into white tin when it is warmed up again. Tin does not react with water, but it will react with strong acids and alkalis, and with oxygen when heated in air.

What are its main uses?   Tin is important in glass making, but its most familiar use is in 'tin' cans for storing food. It is also used in alloys such as solder, bronze and pewter. Most tin **compounds** are toxic, and some are used to prevent barnacles and other sea creatures growing on the hulls of ships.

207 Pb lead 82	**lead** *symbol: Pb • atomic number: 82 • metal*

Lead is an Anglo-Saxon word, but the symbol comes from the Latin word for lead (*plumbum*). Lead metal is only rarely found in its native form as a free element, but like tin it has been known for thousands of years. Galena, lead sulphide, is the most important lead **ore.** Lead is a very soft, shiny, blue-white metal. It is fairly unreactive as it is protected by a thin layer of grey lead oxide.

Lead has many uses including radiation shielding, car batteries, bullets, glass and **insecticides**. Many lead compounds are brightly coloured, and are used in **pigments** and paints. However, lead is poisonous, so it has to be handled carefully.

289 Uuq ununquadium 114	**ununquadium** *symbol: Uuq • atomic number: 114 • metal*

Only a few **atoms** of this metal have been made. Its name means 'one-one-four' and is temporary until scientists know more about the element. Ununquadium was first produced in 1998 by smashing high-speed calcium atoms into plutonium atoms in a machine called a particle accelerator.

Carbon

Three **allotropes** of carbon occur naturally: diamond, graphite and **amorphous** carbon (found in coal, charcoal and soot). These have been known for thousands of years, but it was not until the 18th century that people realized they were all forms of the same **element**.

In 1772 a French chemist, Antoine Lavoisier, showed that diamonds are made of carbon. He weighed samples of amorphous carbon and diamond, carefully burnt them, and then weighed the **products** left behind. Lavoisier found that carbon and diamond both produced the same amount of carbon dioxide when they were burnt. He realized that because carbon dioxide was the only product in both cases, diamond must be made of carbon. A Swedish chemist, Carl Scheele, did a similar experiment in 1779 to show that graphite is also made of carbon.

▲ *Lavoisier is considered one of the greatest experimentalists in chemistry.*

When carbon burns, it reacts with oxygen from the air and produces carbon dioxide. The word equation for this is:

carbon + oxygen → carbon dioxide

Amorphous carbon

Amorphous carbon is a black solid. Soot and charcoal are forms of amorphous carbon, and it is also found in coal. It is formed when substances containing carbon are burnt in a limited supply of oxygen. For example, charcoal is made by burning wood, coconut shells or animal bones.

If charcoal is heated with steam to about 1000 °C while keeping oxygen away, it turns into activated charcoal. This is a very pure form of carbon and it is porous, like a sponge. Chemical **reactions** involving a solid can only happen at its surface, so a solid with a big surface area can react very quickly. The tiny pores in activated charcoal give it a huge surface area, and one gram of it can have the surface area of four tennis courts! It is very good at absorbing other chemicals, so it is used to purify food and water. Cooker hoods often have a filter containing activated charcoal to stop cooking smells escaping into the kitchen.

Amorphous carbon, moulded into shape by putting it under high pressure, is used to make the cores of batteries. However, about 90 per cent of it is used in the rubber industry, mostly for tyres. Carbon gives tyres their familiar black colour, and it also strengthens the rubber so that the tyre is not worn away too quickly. Plastics often have amorphous carbon added to reinforce them, and to protect them from damaging ultraviolet light from the Sun. You will often see this black plastic used for drainpipes and electrical cables.

Amorphous carbon is used in black paints and in the black inks used in ink-jet printers. The toners used in photocopiers and laser printers contain very finely powdered amorphous carbon. As the paper passes through the machine, carbon is baked onto the paper to form the image. Each particle of carbon in the toner can be as small as a hundredth of a millimetre in diameter, which makes very detailed images possible.

The rubber in tyres contains carbon to strengthen it.

Diamond

Pure diamond is a clear and colourless solid, though most diamonds have a faint yellow colour because they contain traces of other **elements**. Diamond is the hardest natural substance known, though it is also very **brittle** and can be smashed with a hammer. It does not conduct electricity, but it is an excellent conductor of heat.

The structure of diamond

Non-metals like carbon join on to other **atoms** using chemical **bonds** called covalent bonds. These bonds form when two atoms share a pair of **electrons**, and every carbon atom can make four covalent bonds. This means that a carbon atom can join to four other atoms using four single covalent bonds, as in methane, CH_4, or to two other atoms using double covalent bonds, as in carbon dioxide, CO_2. In diamond, every carbon atom is joined to four other carbon atoms using single covalent bonds.

A crystal of diamond is a single giant molecule, called a macromolecule. A molecule of diamond contains a huge number of atoms and bonds. A diamond 5 mm in diameter weighs about half a carat, or 0.1 g, and it contains about five thousand billion billion carbon atoms! Diamond is very hard because each bond is strong and there are very many of them. It also has a very high melting point, 3550 °C, because a lot of energy is needed to break all the bonds.

Each carbon atom can make four chemical bonds with other atoms. The bonds are arranged so that they point to the four points of an imaginary three-sided pyramid.

bonds   atom

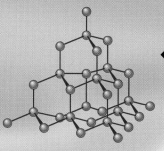

The structure of diamond. Each carbon atom (except the ones at the surface) is joined to four other carbon atoms to make a giant molecule.

Mining and manufacture

Natural diamonds formed underground millions of years ago in molten rock, called magma, under huge pressures and temperatures. As the magma flowed towards the surface through volcanic pipes, it cooled and solidified to form a blue rock called kimberlite. Miners dig this out of the ground to get at the diamonds. Diamonds are found all over the world, but most diamond mines are in South Africa and the Democratic Republic of the Congo.

Artificial diamonds can be made for industrial use. Small diamonds just a few millimetres across are made by dissolving graphite in molten nickel, then heating and squashing it for several hours. Thin films of diamond are made on the surface of other substances by heating carbon to a high temperature at low pressure. This causes the carbon to turn into a vapour, which then reforms as a film of diamond on the surface.

The uses of diamond

Clear diamonds with a good colour are called gem diamonds. Before they can be used for jewellery, they need to be cut to size and shape by highly skilled diamond cutters so that they sparkle in the light. Only about a quarter of mined diamonds are good enough for jewellery – the rest are used with artificial diamonds for industry.

Industrial diamonds are used as hardwearing edges on cutting tools for drilling oil wells. Diamond films are used in electronic devices, where they conduct heat away from computer chips and other components.

Diamonds like these can be used in jewellery. They are often set in precious metals to show off their high quality.

Graphite

Graphite is a **brittle**, shiny black solid. It has a soft, slippery feel and leaves a black mark when rubbed on paper, which means that it can be used in pencils. Like diamond, it does not dissolve in water and it has a high melting point, but unlike diamond it conducts electricity.

The structure of graphite

Graphite consists of layers of carbon **atoms** stacked on top of one another, with very weak **bonds** between them. These bonds are so weak that the layers can slide over each other very easily, which is why graphite is soft and slippery.

The structure of graphite. Each carbon atom in a layer is joined to three other carbon atoms to make hexagonal rings. There are very weak bonds between the layers.

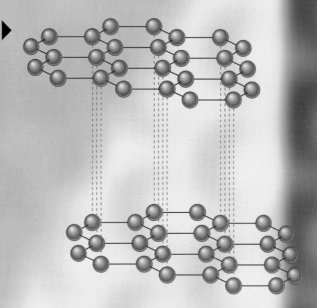

The carbon atoms in a layer of graphite are joined using single covalent bonds. The rings of six atoms are joined so that each layer looks like a honeycomb or a piece of chicken wire. There are 'spare' **electrons** in every layer, because each carbon atom uses only three of the four bonds that it is able to make. These electrons are called delocalized electrons, and they are free to move about in the layer. Graphite conducts electricity because the spare electrons can move and carry electric charge through the graphite. It is very unusual for a non-metal to conduct electricity.

Mining and manufacture

Sticks of lead metal were used to draw on paper until 1564, when a deposit of very pure graphite was found in Borrowdale, England. The graphite was mined, cut into shape and used for pencils. It was so valuable that the mine was only open a few weeks a year, and armed guards followed the wagons carrying the graphite! At the time nobody knew that the substance was a form of carbon, so it was called plumbago, which means 'acts like lead'. Over two hundred years later Carl Scheele discovered that plumbago was made of carbon, not lead. Abraham Werner suggested the name graphite in 1789, from the Greek word that means 'to write'. People still talk about pencil lead, even though it is actually carbon.

Graphite is found in metamorphic rocks such as marble and schist, and world production is about 600,000 tonnes a year. About 41 per cent of the graphite comes from China, much of the remainder comes from India, Brazil and Mexico.

The uses of graphite

Graphite has a very high melting point, so it is used to make the linings for furnaces, brakes for cars and equipment to cast molten steel. It is also used as a heat-resistant lubricant because it is slippery. As it conducts electricity, graphite is used in batteries, motors, and to make the electrodes needed to extract aluminium from its **ore** using electricity. Composite materials containing stiff graphite are used to make carbon-fibre boats, car parts and sports equipment such as fishing rods and golf clubs.

A piece of graphite from a plumbago mine. Graphite is a soft substance that flakes easily and feels greasy.

Fullerenes

Three scientists discovered a new **allotrope** of carbon in 1985. Richard Smalley and Robert Curl from America, and Harold Kroto from Britain, fired a powerful laser at graphite and then analysed the pieces that were blasted off. They detected a molecule made of 60 carbon **atoms**, C_{60}. When they worked out the arrangement of the atoms in this molecule, they found that it was a hollow sphere made of pentagons and hexagons – just like a soccer ball! They called the new molecule buckminsterfullerene, after an American called Richard Buckminster Fuller who designed 'geodesic domes' (buildings that happen to look similar to the molecule). Different types of these molecules have been discovered, and they are called fullerenes for short. The three scientists were awarded the 1996 Nobel Prize in Chemistry for their discovery.

One of Buckminster Fuller's geodesic domes. These domes enclose large volumes using fewer building materials than normal buildings.

Buckyballs

Fullerenes are now made by passing electricity between a pointed graphite rod and a graphite disk. As the electricity jumps between them, it flashes like lightning and makes fine soot. When the soot is dissolved in a liquid called toluene, it makes a red-brown solution of fullerenes. If the solution is filtered and the toluene evaporated, almost pure fullerenes are left behind. The smallest fullerene molecule has 20 carbon atoms, and the largest so far has 540 carbon atoms. They are often called buckyballs because they are made from rounded cages of carbon atoms.

Research into buckyballs has lead to new materials such as diamond films, and they have even been joined together to make **polymers**. With their rounded shape, like tiny ball bearings, buckyballs should make good lubricants.

The space inside buckyballs can contain other substances, such as metal atoms. These buckyballs, called fullerides, can even be shrunk to fit snugly around the metal atom!

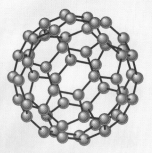

◀ *A model of a buckyball containing 60 carbon atoms. Its faces are hexagons and pentagons.*

One or more of the carbon atoms in the buckyball can be swapped for another **element** to make a huge range of molecules called fulleroids. Scientists are hopeful that these will lead to new **catalysts** and electronic components. Fulleroids containing potassium or rubidium conduct electricity. In fact, they do it so well that at very low temperatures they are superconductors. This means that no energy is lost as heat when they conduct electricity, unlike normal conductors such as copper.

Nanotubes

If buckyballs are opened up, fullerene cylinders called nanotubes are made. These are very tiny tubes, made of carbon, that are thousands of times finer than a human hair. Nanotubes promise to be even more useful than buckyballs as they are six times lighter than steel, but a hundred times stronger. This means that they can be used instead of graphite fibres to make even lighter and stronger materials. It is already possible to buy a nanotube-reinforced tennis racquet. Superconducting nanotubes have been developed, and theoretically they should eventually lead to wires that carry electricity without losing any energy.

▼ *A diagram of part of a nanotube. One million of the finest nanotubes would make a stack only 1 mm high.*

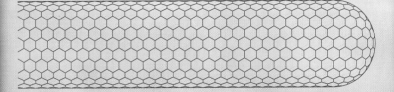

Coal

Coal is a sedimentary rock made from the ancient remains of plants. It is a natural source of **amorphous** carbon. Coal is commonly used as a fuel, especially in power stations, but it is also used to make a wide range of chemicals.

The formation of coal

During the Carboniferous Period, 280 million to 300 million years ago, huge swampy tropical forests covered a lot of the world. When the trees and other plants died, many of them did not rot away as usual because the swampy conditions stopped fungi and micro-organisms feeding on them. Thick deposits of dead plants built up on top of each other and were buried by layers of mud and sand. Over thousands of years, the weight of this mud and sand squashed the buried plants, and chemical **reactions** turned them into coal. A layer of coal is called a seam, and each metre of coal came from about 15 metres of dead plant material.

The word equation for one of the reactions that turns cellulose in plant cell walls into carbon is:

cellulose → carbon + carbon dioxide + methane + water

The carbon dioxide, methane and water gradually escape to leave the carbon behind as coal.

There are different types of coal depending on how long these reactions have been going on. Low-rank coals, such as dark brown lignite, contain the least amount of carbon and have formed relatively recently. High-rank coals, such as shiny black bituminous coal, contain the most carbon. Anthracite is the oldest and best coal of all – over 95 per cent of it is carbon.

The USA and China mine over half of the total of mined black coal. Brown coal is mined mainly by Germany and Greece.

Coal mining

While the coal formed, the mud and sand that covered it turned into sedimentary rocks such as sandstone and shale. The coal seams are found under these rocks. Different methods are used to mine the coal depending upon how deeply it is buried.

Coal seams within 80 metres of the surface are usually removed by open-cast mining. The soil and rock on top of the coal is removed and stored. The coal is dug up using huge machines. Deep pits or strips are dug, depending on the layout of the coal seam and obstacles such as villages. After the coal has been removed, the stored rock and soil is put back. New plants are planted to reduce the damage done to the environment.

If the coal seams are too deep for open-cast mining, shafts are dug down to the coal. Miners dig into the seam (which might only be 1–2 metres deep) and bring the coal to the surface through the mine-shaft. Originally, miners used pickaxes and brute strength to get at the coal, and pit ponies to pull the coal wagons. It was dangerous work, and even children were sent down to work in the coal mines. Modern mines use machines to cut the coal and conveyor belts to transport it.

◀ Anthracite coal, shown here, is formed from fossilized plants from the Carboniferous Period (about 300 million years ago).

Uses of coal

Coal as a fuel

Only 5 per cent of the coal produced is used in homes for cooking and heating. The biggest use of coal is for generating electricity, and coal-fired power stations use 62 per cent of the world's coal production. Crushed coal is burnt in boilers in the power station to produce heat, which is used to boil water to make steam. The steam drives a turbine, which turns a generator to make electricity. These power stations produce a lot of electricity. One of the generating units at Paradise Power Station in Kentucky, USA produces over 1000 megawatts, or 10 billion kilowatt-hours per year. Drax power station in North Yorkshire in the UK (the biggest in Europe) has six generating units that produce a total of 4000 megawatts – enough to run 40 million 100 W light bulbs continuously!

Although coal-fired power stations produce 37 per cent of the world's electricity, they are not very efficient. Only 35 per cent of the energy in the coal is converted into electricity – the rest escapes as heat into the environment. When coal burns, the carbon in it reacts with oxygen in the air to make carbon dioxide. This is a greenhouse gas that traps heat in the atmosphere, causing global warming.

Railway wagons bring coal to be burnt in this coal-fired power station. ▶

Coal contains sulphur impurities that produce sulphur dioxide when the coal is burnt. If this gas escapes into the atmosphere, it dissolves in the water in the clouds to produce acid rain. Coal also contains various **minerals** that leave ash behind, some of which escapes out of chimneys. In modern coal-fired power stations, filters remove most of the sulphur dioxide and ash before they can escape into the atmosphere.

Coal in the chemical industry

If coal is heated very strongly while keeping the air away, it breaks down to make some useful new substances. This process is called **destructive distillation**, and it produces coal gas, coal tar and coke.

Coal gas, sometimes called town gas, is a smelly mixture of gases including methane, carbon monoxide and hydrogen. Town gas was used for heating and lighting before natural gas was discovered. It is still used today as an industrial fuel, and it can be used in metal **refining**.

Coal tar is a mixture of over a hundred different carbon **compounds**, such as benzene and naphthalene. These compounds are separated using **fractional distillation**, and used to make Nylon®, varnish, dyes and paints, explosives, medicines and pesticides. A thick black tar is left over after fractional distillation. This is used to waterproof roofs and to make roads.

Coke is pure carbon and makes a very good fuel. When it burns, it releases more heat than coal and much less smoke. It is also used as a starting material in the chemical industry for making plastics and other substances. Coke is one of the raw materials used in the extraction of iron from iron **ore** in blast furnaces.

Carbon dioxide

Carbon dioxide is a clear colourless gas that is denser than air. There are 2,800 billion tonnes of carbon dioxide in the atmosphere, but it dissolves easily in water and the oceans contain about fifty times more carbon dioxide than the atmosphere.

Combustion

Combustion is the chemical word for burning – the chemical **reaction** that occurs when fuels react with oxygen in the air. Fuels that contain carbon include coal, wood, natural gas and fuels made from crude oil such as petrol and diesel. They all release carbon dioxide when they burn. Coal is made almost entirely of carbon, so it produces the most carbon dioxide when it is burnt. The other fuels also contain hydrogen and other **elements**.

The word equations for combustion are:

1) coal + oxygen ⟶ carbon dioxide
2) fuel + oxygen ⟶ carbon dioxide + water

The second equation works for fuels that also contain hydrogen, such as wood, gas and petrol.

Carbon dioxide stops fuels burning and is used in fire extinguishers. These fire extinguishers are safe to use on electrical fires because they do not use water.

If the supply of oxygen is limited, incomplete combustion happens. Some of the carbon in the fuel is released making the flame smoky and sooty, and some of it reacts with oxygen to produce carbon monoxide instead of carbon dioxide. Carbon monoxide is a poisonous, colourless gas with no smell. Small amounts of it will cause you to fall asleep, and larger amounts can kill you.

Limewater is an alkaline liquid used to detect carbon dioxide. In this experiment the limewater has turned cloudy white, showing that the boy breathed out carbon dioxide.

Respiration

Respiration is the chemical reaction that every cell in our body uses to release energy from food. Without it, we could not get the energy we need for all our body's processes, such as moving, growing and keeping warm.

The word equation for respiration is:

$$glucose + oxygen \rightarrow carbon\ dioxide + water$$

Respiration happens in tiny objects in our cells called mitochondria.

Blood carries waste carbon dioxide to our lungs, where it is expelled when we breathe out. The air we breathe in contains about 0.036 per cent carbon dioxide, but the air we breathe out contains about 3.7 per cent carbon dioxide when we are resting, to more than 5 per cent when we are exercising.

Fermentation

Yeast are microscopic single-celled fungi. They contain **enzymes** that can break up sugar to release energy in a process called **fermentation**.

The word equation for fermentation is:

$$glucose \xrightarrow{\text{enzymes in yeast}} ethanol + carbon\ dioxide$$

Yeast is used in bread making because the carbon dioxide released makes the dough rise. Yeast is also used in making wine and beer because fermentation releases ethanol (alcohol).

More about carbon dioxide

Carbon dioxide is added to drinks under pressure to make them fizzy. When drinks like champagne and cola are opened, the pressure is released and lots of carbon dioxide bubbles escape.

If carbon dioxide is cooled to −78.5 °C it freezes to make a white solid called 'dry ice'. This is used to keep food and medical samples cold while they are transported. As it warms up, dry ice turns back into a gas without becoming a liquid. This process is called subliming. When dry ice sublimes, it makes a white mist that is used for special effects in rock concerts and films.

Dry ice dropped into a beaker of water ▲
makes bubbles and lots of mist that
flows over the edge.

Photosynthesis

Photosynthesis is the chemical **reaction** in plants that produces food by using carbon dioxide, water and energy from sunlight.

The word equation for photosynthesis is:

$$\text{carbon dioxide + water} \xrightarrow{\text{sunlight}} \text{glucose + oxygen}$$

Photosynthesis is carried out in tiny green objects in the plant cells called chloroplasts.

Plants also need to respire. During the day, when there is a lot of sunlight, the rate of photosynthesis is more than the rate of respiration. It is then that plants take in carbon dioxide. However, at night when it is dark, plants cannot photosynthesize and so release carbon dioxide as they respire. Farmers often add extra carbon dioxide to the air if they are growing their crop in greenhouses. This makes the plants photosynthesize faster, so they grow faster and produce more food.

The greenhouse effect

Energy from the Sun passes through the atmosphere and some of it escapes back into space as infrared radiation, or heat. The carbon dioxide in the atmosphere is very good at absorbing infrared radiation, trapping heat in the atmosphere. This is called the greenhouse effect and it keeps the Earth warm. The average surface temperature of our planet is 14 °C, but without the greenhouse effect the Earth would be almost as cold as the Moon, which has an average surface temperature of −18 °C.

Human activities have been adding more carbon dioxide to the atmosphere than can be removed by natural processes. There are two main activities involved. Industrial processes and burning **fossil fuels** produce 65 per cent of the extra carbon dioxide, and cutting down forests for building and farmland produces most of the rest. Fewer trees also mean that less carbon dioxide can be removed by photosynthesis. In 300 years the amount of carbon dioxide in the air has gone up from 0.0275 per cent to 0.0365 per cent. This might not sound a lot, but as the levels have gone up, so has the average temperature at the Earth's surface. Average temperatures have increased about 0.6 °C since the late 19th century. This is called global warming, and it is leading to changing weather patterns. The polar ice caps may melt, causing sea levels to rise and lowland areas to flood.

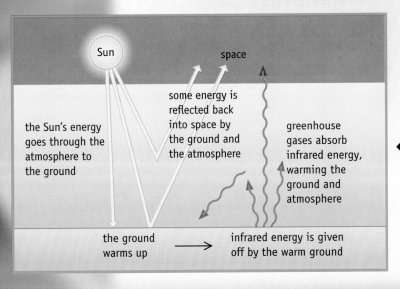

the Sun's energy goes through the atmosphere to the ground

some energy is reflected back into space by the ground and the atmosphere

greenhouse gases absorb infrared energy, warming the ground and atmosphere

the ground warms up → infrared energy is given off by the warm ground

Diagram to show how carbon dioxide traps heat in the atmosphere. Methane from rice fields and flooded land is also a greenhouse gas.

Calcium carbonate

Calcium carbonate is a solid **compound** that contains calcium, carbon and oxygen. Living things in the oceans, such as snails and crabs, can use carbon dioxide dissolved in the water to make calcium carbonate for their shells. Vast numbers of microscopic animals and plants called plankton also make their shells from calcium carbonate. When these living things die, they sink to the seabed to form layers of shells. These layers, called sediments, build up on top of each other and their weight squeezes the water out from between the shells. Over thousands of years, the shells become stuck together by salt crystals to form sedimentary rocks called limestone and chalk.

Chalk

Chalk is a white crumbly rock. Gymnasts and weight-lifters rub it into their hands to get a better grip. Cement is made by roasting a mixture of chalk and clay. Concrete is made by mixing cement, sand, aggregate (small stones) and water together.

Limestone

Limestone is a tough rock that can be used as a building material, and crushed limestone is used in road building. Carbonates, such as the calcium carbonate in limestone, **neutralize** acids by reacting with them to produce a calcium salt, water and carbon dioxide. This can be useful in areas where there is a risk of high amounts of acid rain. Acid rain can pollute lakes, making it difficult for fish and other living things to survive, so powdered limestone may be added to the lakes to neutralize the extra acid.

If limestone is heated, it decomposes (breaks down) to make calcium oxide and carbon dioxide. Calcium oxide is often called lime, and farmers use it to neutralize acid soils to help their crops grow better. Mortar, used by builders to join bricks together to make walls, is made by mixing lime with sand and water. When iron is being made from iron **ore** in the blast furnace, it contains sandy impurities. Calcium oxide from heated limestone reacts with these impurities to make a slag, which is then easily removed leaving pure iron.

Marble

If limestone is buried deep underground by Earth movements, it gets squashed and heated, and turns into a metamorphic rock called marble. This is shiny and harder than limestone or chalk. It can be polished to an attractive finish and is used for statues, kitchen and bathroom surfaces and as a decorative cladding on buildings.

Acid attacks rock

Calcium carbonate reacts with acid and dissolves away. Rain is naturally acidic because carbon dioxide dissolves in it to make carbonic acid. Over thousands of years, the acid in rain and rivers dissolves limestone and chalk to form caves. When water drips from the roof of a cave, it evaporates to leave columns of calcium carbonate behind. These are called stalactites and stalagmites. Air pollution has made rain more acidic than normal, which is badly damaging statues and buildings made from limestone or marble.

◀ Acid in rainwater has reacted with limestone to form this cave. The columns of calcium carbonate hanging from the ceiling are called stalactites, and the ones extending upwards are called stalagmites.

Oil and natural gas

Oil and natural gas contain **compounds** of hydrogen and carbon called **hydrocarbons**. They are used widely as fuels, but they are also used to make **products** such as plastics, dyes and cosmetics. The oil and natural gas on Earth will eventually run out and so they are called non-renewable energy resources.

The formation of oil and natural gas

Millions of years ago, sea creatures died, sank to the seabed and were covered by layers of mineral sediments. The sediments and the remains of the dead creatures were buried deeper and deeper. Oxygen could not get to the remains, so they did not rot away. Instead, they heated up and were squashed by the weight of the sediments. Eventually, the **mineral** sediments turned into rock, and the remains turned into oil and gas. Water pushed the oil and gas upwards through **permeable rock** (rock with holes and cracks like a sponge) and when they reached **impermeable rock**, they could not rise any further and were trapped.

▲ *Crude oil is not at all like the engine oil you see used in cars. It is thick, black and very smelly.*

Drilling for oil

Oil workers drill deep into the ground and through the layer of impermeable rock to get at oil and gas. Natural gas is usually found just below the impermeable rock, and oil further down. Once it is out of the ground, a pipeline or tanker sends the oil to an oil refinery.

Oil refining

At the oil refinery, oil is separated into different hydrocarbons by a process called **fractional distillation**. The oil is heated to about 350 °C and pumped into the bottom of a tall metal tower called a fractionating column. The column is very hot at the bottom, and vapours from the heated oil rise up the column towards the top where it is colder.

Hydrocarbons with a lot of carbon **atoms** have very high boiling points. They remain solid at 350 °C, so they just stay at the bottom of the column. Hydrocarbons with fewer than five carbon atoms in them are gases. They have low boiling points and so are able to make it right to the top without condensing into a liquid. The vapours from the medium-sized hydrocarbons rise until they get cool enough to condense back into a liquid. The liquids are collected in trays inside the column and piped away.

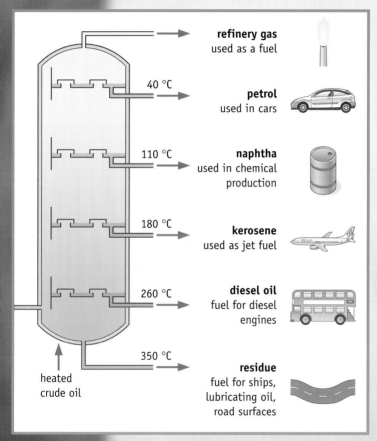

refinery gas
used as a fuel

40 °C

petrol
used in cars

110 °C **naphtha**
used in chemical
production

180 °C **kerosene**
used as jet fuel

260 °C **diesel oil**
fuel for diesel
engines

350 °C

residue
fuel for ships,
lubricating oil,
road surfaces

heated
crude oil

The different parts separated from the oil are called fractions. The fractions at the bottom of the column are solids with big molecules, those in the middle are liquids with medium-sized molecules, and the fractions at the top are gases with very small molecules.

The main oil fractions from a fractionating column.

Cracking

Crude oil often contains too many big molecules but not enough of the more useful medium-sized molecules, like petrol. The big molecules are converted into smaller molecules by using a catalyst or by heating them strongly under pressure. This process is called cracking, and it is important because some of the smaller molecules are useful to the chemical industry and can be used to make plastics.

Complex molecules

Carbon **atoms** can form four **bonds** with other atoms, including carbon itself. This means that carbon atoms can join together to make chains and rings of carbon atoms, with other **elements** joined on in countless different ways. Living things produce large and complex molecules by joining small molecules together. Chemists have learnt how to copy this and make synthetic materials such as plastics and medicines.

Plastics

When oil fractions are cracked in the refinery, **alkenes** are made. Alkenes contain two or more carbon atoms joined by double covalent bonds, and they can join end to end to make very long molecules called addition **polymers**. Lots of addition polymers are possible. For example, ethene molecules can join end to end to make poly(ethene), which is used to make polythene bags; propene molecules make poly(propene), which is used to make tough polypropylene ropes; and styrene molecules make poly(styrene), which is used for fast-food containers and television cabinets.

▼ *All these products are from polymers – long complex carbon compounds made from lots of small molecules called monomers.*

Carbohydrates

Carbohydrates such as sugar and starch are naturally occurring **compounds** of carbon, hydrogen and oxygen. Two molecules of a simple sugar can join together to make more complex sugars. Sucrose (cane sugar) is made from glucose and fructose joined together, and lactose (found in milk) is made from glucose and galactose. Thousands of glucose molecules can join together to make starch (found in rice and bread) or cellulose, depending on how they are joined. Cellulose is the tough molecule found in plant cell walls.

Polyesters

Fats and oils are made from two carbon compounds, glycerol (a type of alcohol) and fatty acids. The fatty acids join on to the glycerol using a type of chemical bond called an ester bond. Chemists can make polymers called polyesters because they contain lots of ester bonds. Polyester can be used to make bottles and videotape. Polyester fibres, such as Terylene®, are used to make soft, hardwearing clothes.

DNA

DNA stands for deoxyribonucleic acid, which is a long name and often a very long molecule. A single DNA molecule can be 7 cm long, and each human cell contains 2 m of it tightly coiled to fit inside the **nucleus**! DNA contains the genetic code for producing all the different proteins a cell needs, and human DNA contains at least 30,000 genes. DNA is made from four different carbon compounds called nucleotides, which can join together in countless combinations.

Proteins and tights

Proteins are large molecules made from small carbon compounds called amino acids. Amino acids join on to each other using a type of chemical bond called a peptide bond. Polyamides contain the same sort of bond. Polyamides, such as Nylon®, are used to make ropes, shirts and ladies' tights.

The carbon cycle

How many carbon **atoms** are there in your body? If you have a mass of 60 kg, your body will contain around 14 kg of carbon. That's about 690 million billion billion carbon atoms, and there's a chance that one of those atoms could once have been part of a famous scientist like Mendeleev, or a prehistoric plant! This is because different processes continually recycle carbon between the atmosphere and the other substances that contain carbon – including you!

Processes that remove carbon dioxide from the atmosphere

In the process of **photosynthesis** green plants take in carbon dioxide from the atmosphere and make glucose from it. This is used to make starch, cellulose, proteins, fats and all the other complex molecules a plant needs to stay alive. Carbon dioxide from the atmosphere dissolves easily in water to form carbonic acid and metal carbonates. Some of this is used by sea creatures to build their shells, which eventually become sedimentary rocks such as chalk and limestone. This is another example where carbon dioxide from the atmosphere enters into the processes of living things.

Processes that return carbon dioxide to the atmosphere

Plants and animals respire as they use energy from their food, and this returns carbon dioxide to the atmosphere. It's a strange thought, but the energy we use to move or grow was originally sunlight, captured by the green chlorophyll in plant leaves. When animals and plants die, other organisms feed on them and they also respire. If dead things did not decay, we would quickly be knee-deep in them! Some dead animals and plants form **fossil fuels** instead of decaying, and these release carbon dioxide when they are burnt. The energy released when we burn coal, oil or natural gas was originally sunlight, captured by plants millions of years ago. Carbon dioxide is also released when limestone is used in the manufacture of cement and iron.

Global warming

Gases such as carbon dioxide and methane trap heat in the atmosphere, causing the Earth to warm up. The carbon cycle should be balanced, but it is not. Human activities are releasing more carbon dioxide than can be used up naturally, causing global warming. Large amounts of carbon dioxide are released when fossil fuels are burnt, but clearing and burning forests for farmland adds to the problem. This is because the burning trees release carbon dioxide and there are fewer trees left for photosynthesis.

▼ *This is the carbon cycle. It shows how carbon in all sorts of compounds is recycled.*

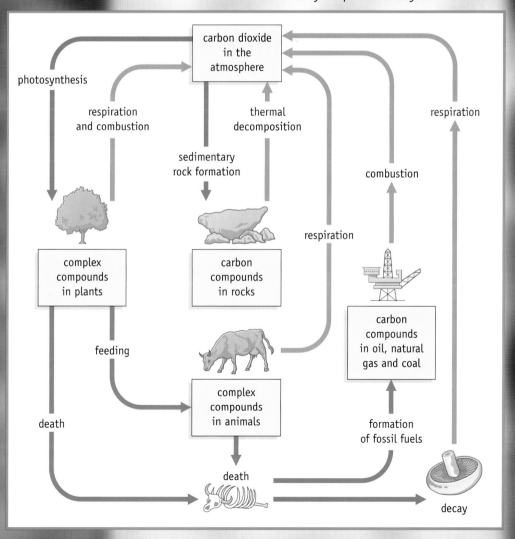

Silicon

Silicon makes up 25.7 per cent of the Earth's crust and is the second most abundant **element** in it. However, it was not discovered until 1823 because it is not found as a free element. Instead, silicon is usually found joined with oxygen to make silicon dioxide, also called silica. Quartz is made from silica, and it is the most common **mineral** in sand. Silicon is also found joined with other elements as well as oxygen to make silicates. There are more than 1000 silicates, including talc, clay and asbestos. Silicon is widely used in electronic devices, and silicon **compounds** are used in concrete, brick, pottery, glass and silicone sealants. Silicon carbide (carborundum) is the next hardest substance after diamond and is used to make cutting tools.

The structure of silicon

There are two forms or **allotropes** of silicon. **Amorphous** silicon is a red-brown powder that does not conduct electricity. Crystalline silicon is a shiny grey-black solid that conducts electricity, though not as well as a metal. The structure of crystalline silicon is very similar to the structure of diamond. A crystal of crystalline silicon is a single giant molecule, with every silicon **atom** joined on to four other silicon atoms using covalent **bonds**. As each bond is strong and there are very many of them, silicon is hard and has a high melting point, 1410 °C.

Silicon is fairly unreactive. It does not react with water or most acids, but it will react with steam and alkalis. It will also react with oxygen to make silicon dioxide or silica. This exists in two forms, crystalline silica such as quartz, and amorphous silica such as opal.

The manufacture of silicon

There are three stages in the manufacture of silicon. Sand (silicon dioxide) is the usual starting material and the end result is a fairly pure form of the element. However, this is not pure enough for the **semi-conductor** materials used to make 'silicon chips'. A process called **zone refining** is used to make hyperpure silicon for electronic circuits.

▲ *These huge sand dunes contain countless grains of sand, a compound of silicon and oxygen.*

The reactions in the extraction of silicon are:

In the first stage, the oxygen is removed from the sand by heating it with coke (a cheap type of pure carbon) to leave impure silicon behind. The word equation for the first stage in making silicon is:

silicon dioxide + carbon → silicon + carbon dioxide

The silicon made at this stage is impure. In the second stage, the impure silicon is reacted with chlorine gas to make a liquid called silicon tetrachloride. This is purified using **fractional distillation**.

The word equation for the second stage in making silicon is:

silicon + chlorine → silicon tetrachloride

In the third stage, the pure silicon tetrachloride is reacted with hydrogen to make silicon. The word equation for the third stage in making silicon is:

silicon tetrachloride + hydrogen → silicon + hydrogen chloride

Bunny and chips

Computer chips and other electronic devices are made from **semi-conductors**. These are substances, such as silicon, that are electrical insulators at room temperature, but conductors when they are warmed up. They also conduct when tiny amounts of other **elements** are added to them. This process is called doping. If silicon is doped with phosphorus or arsenic it makes 'N-type silicon'. Electrical charge moves through N-type silicon using **electrons**, which are negatively charged. If silicon is doped with boron or gallium it makes 'P-type silicon', and electrical charge moves through it using positively charged 'holes'. The millions of transistors in computer chips are made from both types of doped silicon.

Wafers in a 'clean room'

Computer chips start as very pure silicon called hyperpure silicon. Single crystals of hyperpure silicon are made into rods up to 30 cm in diameter, then sliced into circular wafers

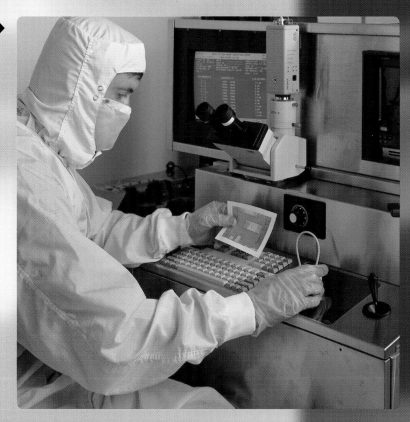

A technician, seated at a microscope in a 'clean room', holds a photograph of part of a silicon wafer while checking on its microcircuit.

only 0.5 mm thick using a diamond saw. The wafers are polished flat and checked for scratches. It is very important that dust does not get on to the wafers while the electronic components are being made on them. Even one speck of dust could make a computer chip useless, For this reason the chips are made in a 'clean room'.

A cubic metre of ordinary air contains millions of dust particles, but the air in a 'clean room' contains fewer than forty specks of dust in a cubic metre of air. To stop dust, skin and hair getting into the room, everyone working in there must wear special protective clothing called a **bunny suit**. This is worn over normal clothes, and it includes a helmet with a battery-powered air filter, a hair net, two layers of nylon and latex gloves, and two layers of overshoes. Even beards have to be covered up!

Chip building

Lots of chips are made on a single wafer. A typical chip might contain 20 layers, each with a complex pattern of lines and shapes etched in silicon. Chip designers make a set of special stencils called masks, and each mask has the pattern for one layer. Ultraviolet light is used to transfer the pattern from a mask on to the wafer in a process called **photolithography**. Different chemicals are used to shape the layer and to dope the silicon. The process is repeated with different masks to build up the layers, one on top of the other.

Copper and aluminium are added to conduct electricity from one part of the chip to another. Each chip is tested while it is still on the wafer, then the wafer is carefully cut up into separate chips using a diamond saw. Each chip is put into a plastic case to protect it, and very fine gold wires are used to connect it to circuit boards.

Super sand

Sand is largely made up of crystalline silicon dioxide. It is used in concrete and mortar, and to make sandpaper. Dirty buildings can be cleaned by blasting sharp sand through a hose using compressed air. Finely powdered sand is used in paints, plastics and **ceramics**. Sand mixed with clay is used to make bricks, and moulds for casting metal. Pure sand is used to line furnaces because it is heat-resistant, but the biggest single use for sand is in making glass. About 38 per cent of the 107,000 tonnes of sand used in the world each year is used in this way.

Making glass

If sand is melted then cooled slowly, it turns back into solid crystals of sand. However, if the liquid sand is cooled very quickly, it solidifies before the crystals can form, and glass is made instead. Volcanic eruptions often provide the conditions needed for glass to form naturally, and prehistoric people used glass made this way to make tools. Man-made glass was first produced about 6000 years ago.

Mouth blowing was the main method of forming glass objects for nearly 2000 years until machines took over in the last century. The glass blower shapes the glass by turning the pipe continuously, blowing air into the glass, and using a wet graphite mould.

Glass can be made from sand on its own, however, there are two problems: a very high temperature is needed and the resulting glass melts in water. If sodium carbonate is added to the sand, the melting temperature is reduced from 1700 °C to about 800 °C. If calcium carbonate and magnesium carbonate are added to the glass while it is molten, this prevents it from dissolving. Glass made in this way is called soda-lime glass or bottle glass. Unfortunately, it shatters easily if hot liquids touch it.

Borosilicate glass does not shatter easily when heated because it contains other chemicals, such as boric acid. This glass is used in laboratories, fibre glass, and heat-resistant cooking bowls. Aluminosilicate glass contains about 20 per cent aluminium oxide. It is more heat-resistant than borosilicate glass, so it is used in halogen lamps, which become very hot indeed. Glass ceramics are particularly heat resistant, so they are used for cooker hobs and missile nose cones.

Lead crystal glass contains at least 24 per cent lead oxide. It can be cut and engraved easily to make attractive glassware. Although lead compounds are poisonous, they are trapped in the glass and there is usually little chance of being poisoned when drinking from it. Glass with a lot of lead oxide (over 65 per cent) is used for radiation shielding.

Silicosis

Tiny particles of silica from sand can cause a lung disease called silicosis. The lungs of someone who breathes in silica dust over a long time develop scars and tough bumps called nodules. If the nodules get too big, it becomes difficult to breathe and the victim may die. To avoid these dangers, workers have to take precautions to prevent breathing in any silica. This is serious in jobs such as sandblasting, drilling and blasting rock or concrete, demolition of buildings, and mining.

Diatomite, silicates and silicones

Diatomite

Diatoms are tiny single-celled plants that live in rivers, lakes and seas. They are so small that 25 million of them could fit into a teaspoon! They are extremely useful to us because they make their shells from silica. When they die, their shells sink and form a sedimentary rock called diatomite. This rock is largely made up of **amorphous** silica, along with some other chemicals. About 2 million tonnes of diatomite are used every year, mostly for filtering beer, oil, medicines and swimming pool water. It is also used in paints, plastic, rubber and paper and for making silicates. Diatomite is very good at absorbing liquids, and is used for all sorts of purposes, from soaking up chemical spills to cat litter!

Silicates

Silicon dioxide will not dissolve in water – try dissolving some sand in a beaker of water as an experiment. However, it reacts with sodium hydroxide (a common alkali) to make sodium silicate, which does dissolve in water. Sodium silicate is a solid containing sodium, silicon and oxygen. It is often called 'water glass', and you will have come across it if you have made a 'crystal garden' at home or school.

There are other silicates that do not dissolve in water. Calcium silicate is used for heat insulation and sound insulation. Magnesium silicate is a soft and slippery solid, often called French chalk or talc. It is the main ingredient in talcum powder, and it is also used in soap, paint and fireproof materials. If you have ever had a tooth filled by the dentist, zirconium silicate might be an ingredient in your filling.

Zeolites are porous solids made from aluminosilicates (these are silicates that contain aluminium). Natural zeolites are mainly used in cat litter and can also be used to turn hard water into soft water by a process called ion exchange. Hard water contains calcium or magnesium salts that make it difficult to get soap to lather. Zeolites soften the water by removing these salts. Man-made zeolites are used as **catalysts** in oil refineries to crack oil fractions.

Slippery silicones

Silicones were discovered in 1904 by an English chemist, Frederick Kipping. These are **compounds** that contain long chains of silicon and oxygen **atoms**, with carbon and hydrogen atoms attached to them. Silicones are colourless, unreactive substances that repel water (they don't get wet). This means that they are very useful for waterproofing clothes and for sealing the edges around baths and showers. Some silicones are oily liquids used in cosmetics, while others are used to lubricate moving parts and to conduct heat away in machinery. Some silicones do not squash easily, so are used as hydraulic fluid in car braking systems. Silicones can also be made into the rubbery solids used in cosmetic surgery.

◄ *A 'crystal garden' in a solution of 'water glass'. Crystals of metal salts such as copper sulphate are dropped into the 'water glass', and left for about a week. Coloured hollow tubes made from metal silicates grow and branch from the original crystals.*

Germanium

During the 18th and 19th centuries chemists were particularly busy discovering new **elements**. To make things easier for themselves, chemists desperately needed a way to put all the elements into some sort of order. It was a bit like attempting to do a difficult jigsaw puzzle without a picture to help you!

In 1829, a German chemist called Johann Döbereiner spotted that some elements had similar properties to each other. He was able to put these elements into groups of three, which he called triads. However, chemists kept finding new elements which did not fit the triad pattern.

By 1863 the number of elements identified totalled 56. At this point, an English chemist called John Newlands began to organize the elements. He put them in order of their atomic weight (how heavy their **atoms** were compared to each other), and then put them into rows of seven elements. Newlands found that for many elements, the eighth element that followed it behaved in a similar way. He called his discovery the 'Law of Octaves'. Unfortunately, his law did not work for all the elements and many scientists just mocked his ideas. Throughout this time chemists were finding even more elements, all of which needed to be ordered.

Dimitri Mendeleev spent much of his life in St Petersburg, Russia, where you can see his statue and a wall showing his periodic table.

Six years later, Dimitri Mendeleev published his first **periodic table**, which he updated in 1871. Mendeleev arranged the elements in order of their atomic weight, just as Newlands had done, but he did two important things that made his table work. He realized that as so many new elements had been discovered, there must be many others waiting to be found. Mendeleev left gaps for undiscovered elements in his periodic table. From their positions in his table he also bravely predicted what they should be like. One of the gaps he left was between silicon and tin. Mendeleev called the missing element ekasilicon, which means below silicon. He predicted that ekasilicon's properties would be between those of silicon and tin.

In 1886, a German chemist called Clemens Winkler discovered a new element in an **ore** called argyrodite. He called this germanium – it was the real ekasilicon. The properties of germanium were very close to the properties that Mendeleev had predicted fifteen years earlier.

Property	ekasilicon	germanium
colour	grey	grey–white
atomic weight	73.4	72.3
density of the element (g/cm^3)	5.5	5.47
density of the oxide (g/cm^3)	4.7	4.7
boiling point of the chloride (°C)	less than 100	86

▲ *This table shows some of Mendeleev's predicted properties for ekasilicon and the real properties of germanium. Germanium's melting point was 158 °C higher than Mendeleev predicted, but his other predictions were incredibly close.*

Support for new ideas in science comes from making a prediction, based on good scientific reason, that then comes true. This meant that the discovery of germanium was a great success for Mendeleev's periodic table. Our modern periodic table is based closely on his table.

Manufacture and uses of germanium

Germanium is a shiny grey-white solid that is hard, but easily shattered. Germanium is found combined with other **elements**, rather than on its own as a free element. Clemens Winkler discovered germanium in argyrodite (a compound of germanium, sulphur and silver), but the main **ore** is germanite (a compound of germanium, sulphur, copper and iron). Germanium is extracted from germanium oxide using a similar method to the one used to extract silicon. About 58 tonnes are produced every year.

Germanium and the discovery of the transistor

In the middle of the last century, vacuum tubes were used to make, control and amplify electrical signals in electronic equipment. These were not very convenient because they were large, fragile and took time to warm up before they could be used. Modern equipment uses transistors instead because they are much smaller, tougher and do not need to warm up. Three American physicists, John Bardeen, Walter Brattain and William Shockley, invented the first transistor in 1947. This was made from germanium which, like silicon, is a **semi-conductor**. The first integrated circuit (a sort of simple computer chip) was built on to a piece of germanium in 1958. This was difficult to do and most modern chips use silicon instead. Germanium is still used in transistors and in high-power electronics. This is no longer its biggest use – about half of the germanium produced is used for optical fibres.

Germanium and light

Optical fibres are very thin glass tubes, often just an eighth of a millimetre thick. They consist of an inner core of glass surrounded by an outer layer of glass. Light shone into one end will pass through to the other end with very little being lost on the way, because light can travel through the core but is stopped from escaping out of the sides by the outer layer. This process works because the glass in the core contains germanium. Germanium increases the 'refractive index' of the glass and causes light to be reflected back into the core at the join between the core and the outer layer.

Endoscopes are tubes containing optical fibres. Endoscopes let doctors see inside their patients without surgery, and engineers inspect the inside of machinery without taking it apart. Optical fibres are used in long-distance telephone lines and computer networks cables. Signals are sent through them as pulses of infrared light in digital code. So little light is lost on the way that amplifiers (called repeaters) are often only needed every 100 km.

Crystals of bismuth germanate are used in gamma ray detectors because they glow when hit by radiation. Magnesium germanate is used in fluorescent lights because it glows when hit by ultraviolet light.

▲ *Cables containing bundles of optical fibres like these carry large amounts of information, such as telephone conversations and computer data.*

Tin

Ordinary tin is called white tin or β-tin (beta-tin). It is a soft, silvery-white metal with a bluish tinge. When it is bent, crystals in the metal break and you hear a noise called tin cry. If white tin is cooled below 13.2 °C, it gradually changes into another **allotrope** of tin called grey tin or α-tin (alpha tin). This is powdery and not very effective.
The change from white to grey tin is often called tin pest, because people used to think that the devil or microbes caused it!

Tin pest was one of the reasons why Napoleon's 1812 campaign against Moscow failed. Napoleon bought a million greatcoats from England for his troops, and to save money he ordered tin buttons instead of brass ones. The buttons turned into grey tin and crumbled away in the cold Russian winter, making his troops more uncomfortable than they already were. Modern tin usually contains small amounts of bismuth or antimony to stop it turning into grey tin.

These engine houses in the closed Botallack tin mines in Cornwall were once used to pump out flooding water. Being close to sea level lessened the height needed for pumping, so old engine houses are often found perched on cliff tops.

Tin smelting

Each year 200,000 tonnes of tin are produced in the world.
Tin is not found in its native form as a free **element**, but it
has been known for thousands of years because it is easy to
extract from its **ore**. The main ore is cassiterite, which is tin
oxide. This is mined in many countries, although China,
Indonesia and Peru are the main producers. Extracting tin
from its ore is called smelting.

The reactions in the extraction of tin are:

*Crushed cassiterite is heated to about 600 °C to remove
any trapped sulphur impurities. It is then heated to about
1350 °C and stirred with coke for about 15 hours.*

The word equation for smelting tin is:

tin oxide + carbon → tin + carbon dioxide

*Coke or anthracite coal is used to provide the carbon.
Carbon is more reactive than tin, so it removes the oxygen
from the tin oxide. This sort of reaction is called a
displacement reaction.*

*A slag containing impurities eventually floats on a pool of
molten tin, and so can be removed. The tin is poured into
moulds, cooled and solidified. It is then purified or refined
to remove impurities.*

Refining tin

The most common method of **refining** tin is called fire-
refining. The tin is heated to about 1200 °C in a vacuum.
At this temperature, the tin melts and many of its impurities
boil away to leave tin that is up to 99.85 per cent pure.
If very pure tin is needed, electricity can be used to remove
the impurities in a process called **electrolysis**. Tin refined
this way can be 99.9999 per cent pure!

Tin coatings and food cans

If tin is heated with steam or air it reacts to make tin oxide, but it will not react with water or air at room temperature. This makes it very useful for coating other metals to stop them corroding. Tin has a low melting point (232 °C), which means that metal objects can be coated just by dipping them in a bath of molten tin. Tin coatings stick very well and do not easily flake off, even when the object is bent or stretched.

Tinplate is steel coated with a thin layer of tin, often just a thousandth of a millimetre thick, by using a process called electroplating. The steel is dipped in a bath of tin chloride or tin sulphate solution and electricity passed through. This causes a layer of tin to form on the surface of the steel. About 30 per cent of the tin produced is used in tinplate, and nearly all of this goes to make food cans. Thin steel is used in modern cans, but the first cans were so thick that a hammer and chisel were needed to open them!

The Liberty Bell in Philadelphia, USA, was originally cast in 18th-century Britain. Its metallic composition consists of 70 per cent copper, 25 per cent tin, small amounts of lead, zinc, cassiterite, gold and silver, with traces of antimony and nickel.

Alloys and alloy coatings

Tin is used in a large number of alloys, such as solder. This is an **alloy** of tin and lead. It has a low melting point and it is used to make electrical connections. Pewter is used to make attractive tableware, such as drinking goblets and candlesticks. Traditional pewter contains lead, but modern pewter is mostly tin with small amounts of copper, bismuth and antimony to harden the tin. Different bronzes can be made by varying the basic mixture of tin and copper, or by adding other metals.

Metals can be coated with tin alloys for protection and decoration. Tin and nickel alloy coatings resist corrosion very well, and are used for scientific equipment.

Glass-making

Flat glass is made though the float glass process. Molten glass is spread over liquid tin at about 1000 °C. The surface of the tin is flat, so the glass becomes flat too. The molten glass is moved along over the surface of the tin and gradually cooled. When it gets to about 600 °C, it is hard enough to be lifted out and cut to size.

Compounds of tin

Tin oxide is added to glass to make it tougher. Thick layers of tin oxide conduct electricity when sprayed on to glass, and are used to make de-icing panels in car windows. Tin chloride is used as a mordant, which is a chemical that helps a dye stick to cloth.

Compounds containing tin, carbon and other elements are called organotins. Some are very poisonous, such as tributyl tin, which makes it useful as an ingredient in wood preservatives, **fungicides**, and paints for the hulls of ships. Others are not poisonous, and are added to polyvinyl chloride (PVC) to improve its properties.

Lead

Lead is a very soft, blue-white metal. Although graphite is sometimes called black lead it contains carbon, not lead. White lead is actually a range of lead **compounds** that are white in colour. Lead often looks dull grey because its surface reacts quickly with oxygen from the air to form a thin layer of lead oxide. This layer protects the metal below from reacting with any more oxygen, unless the lead is heated above 600 °C. It also stops lead reacting with water or sulphuric acid. For this reason, lead has been used in the past to make water pipes – some ancient Roman pipes even work today! Lead and its compounds are very poisonous, which can cause problems when producing and using it. Lead has a high density, so even small pieces feel heavy.

Each year, 5 million tonnes of lead are produced worldwide. In its native form lead is not found as a free **element**, but, because it is easy to extract from its **ore**, it has been known for thousands of years. The main ore is galena, which is lead sulphide. This is mined in many countries, with the majority of production taking place in Australia and China.

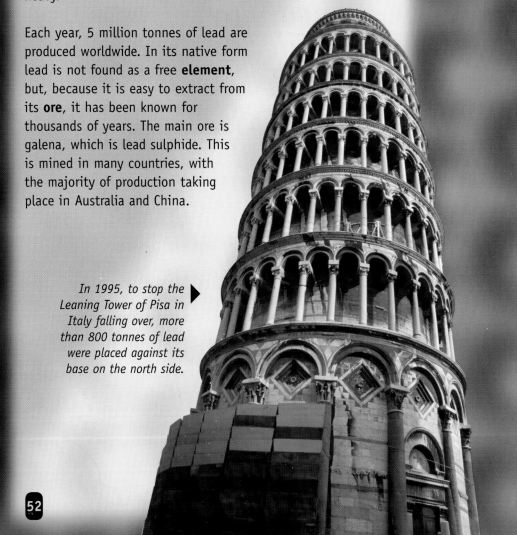

In 1995, to stop the Leaning Tower of Pisa in Italy falling over, more than 800 tonnes of lead were placed against its base on the north side. ▶

Lead smelting

Galena is crushed to a fine powder, then treated by a process called flotation separation to remove any waste rock. The powder is mixed with water and special chemicals. Lots of air is bubbled quickly through the mixture to make a froth that floats on the surface, just like a rocky milk shake! The unwanted rock sinks to the bottom, while the froth containing lead sulphide and other metal compounds is piped off.

The froth is dried and mixed with limestone, then heated to about 1400 °C in a limited supply of air. This removes the sulphur from the lead sulphide and turns it into sulphur dioxide.

The word equation for roasting lead ore is:

lead sulphide + oxygen → lead oxide + sulphur dioxide

The sulphur dioxide is used to make sulphuric acid, which is very important for making **fertilizers** *and explosives.*

Lead oxide is made at this stage, but it is impure and it forms solid lumps called sinter. The sinter is crushed and heated in a furnace to about 1200 °C with carbon monoxide. This removes the oxygen from the lead oxide to make molten lead.

The word equation for reducing lead oxide is:

lead oxide + carbon monoxide → lead + carbon dioxide

The carbon monoxide is made by heating coke in a blast of hot air.

Lead from the furnace is more than 95 per cent pure and is called base bullion. This is purified by a number of complex processes to make lead ready for sale.

Lead the poisoner

Although lead has many uses there is a problem with it. Lead is very poisonous and even tiny amounts of it can harm us. It causes very bad stomach pains if it is breathed in or swallowed. The victim becomes pale and moody, and later their nerves become damaged, causing paralysis. Children can suffer brain damage and may become deaf or blind. People can die from lead poisoning and in the modern world strict laws control the use of lead to protect us. In the past, however, this was not the case.

Sugar of lead

Lead ethanoate tastes sweet, so it is often called sugar of lead. The ancient Romans did not have sugar, but liked sweet food and drink and so used sugar of lead as a sweetener. They made this by leaving sour wine or concentrated grape juice in lead containers. Ethanoic acid in the sour wine or grape juice reacted with the lead to make lead ethanoate. Unfortunately, Romans who liked sweet food suffered from lead poisoning as a result.

Devonshire Colic

Cider is an alcoholic drink made by fermenting apple juice. During the 18th century, cider drinkers in the English county of Devon suffered terrible stomach pains, constipation and other unpleasant symptoms. People thought that sour apples caused the illness, but in 1769 a doctor called George Baker found that it was caused by the lead-lined presses and containers used to make the cider. The drinkers were being poisoned because the cider contained large amounts of lead. Once the lead was removed from the cider-making equipment, Devonshire Colic disappeared.

Gloss paint

White gloss paint used to contain lead **compounds** such as lead silicate and lead carbonate as this made the colour seem pure. If the paint was worn away or peeled off, it became a potential health hazard, and young children were particularly at risk. This is because they like to put objects in their mouth and consequently suffered more from lead poisoning. Modern gloss paints do not contain added lead, and as a result lead poisoning from gloss paint is now rare.

Leaded petrol

When the petrol in a car engine burns too quickly, the engine rattles or 'knocks'. Anti-knocking substances slow down the burning and help the engine run better. The most common anti-knocking substance in the last century was tetraethyl lead, which was first used in petrol in 1923. Unfortunately, the fumes from the exhaust pipes contained lead and over 90 per cent of the lead in the air in cities used to come from leaded petrol. Children in particular were poisoned by the lead, and it also damaged the catalytic converters in cars. As a result, many countries have now banned leaded petrol. The US introduced unleaded petrol in 1976, and by 1990 most petrol sold was unleaded. The UK banned leaded petrol in 2000, and now it can only be used in old classic cars which cannot run on unleaded petrol.

◀ *Homes built before the middle of the last century were often decorated with gloss paint containing lead pigments. There is a bigger chance of being poisoned by the lead if it is peeling off, as seen here.*

Lead in the modern world

Lead does not react with water, so it is used as a roofing material and as a protective covering for underground electricity cables. Lead is used in solders to join electronic components together and in some coloured glazes for **ceramics**. The biggest single use for lead is in the manufacture of batteries for cars and other vehicles.

Strict laws control the use of lead to make sure we are not poisoned by it. Modern products that meet the regulations are unlikely to cause lead poisoning because the lead is sealed inside plastic or glass. However, tiny amounts of lead may still escape, so children and pregnant women are usually advised not to eat or drink from lead-glazed crockery. Hot liquids, and acidic foods such as orange juice and wine, cause more lead to escape from their containers, For this reason, wine should not be stored in lead crystal glassware.

Car batteries

Gaston Planté invented the lead-acid accumulator in 1860. This is the rechargeable battery used in many vehicles, including cars, lorries, forklift trucks and golf buggies. Lead-acid accumulators are filled with 33 per cent sulphuric acid, and they contain plates made of lead and lead oxide. Nearly 80 per cent of the lead produced is used to make these batteries, but over 1 million tonnes of battery lead is recycled each year in the US alone!

A dense metal

Lead is a dense metal, which means that even small objects made from lead are heavy. A litre of milk has a mass of about 1 kg, but a litre of lead has a mass of 11.34 kg! Divers would find it very difficult to stay underwater comfortably without lead weights, and anglers use lead weights to make their fishing lines sink. However, any lead left behind by anglers contaminates the water and may be swallowed by birds. To stop wildlife being poisoned, many places only allow lead-free fishing tackle. Lead is used to make shotgun pellets and bullets, but lead poisoning is rarely a problem in this use of the metal.

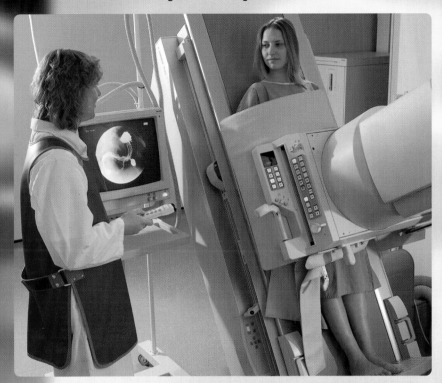

▼ *This patient is being X-rayed. Lead is a very dense metal that will stop radiation. Lead aprons protect patients and staff from getting too much radiation during X-ray photographs. You can even get lead-lined gloves and underwear.*

Lead absorbs radiation very well, so the containers used to transport and store radioactive chemicals are lined with it. Equipment that makes radiation, such as X-ray equipment in hospitals, is shielded by lead. Hospital radiographers, and other people who use radiation in their work, wear aprons containing lead to protect themselves from the harmful effects of radiation.

Glass containing over 65 per cent lead oxide is also used for radiation shielding, with the added advantage that you can see through it! Television tubes produce small amounts of X-rays in normal use, so television sets, computer screens and radar displays use leaded glass to stop the X-rays leaking. Lead crystal glass, which contains about 24 per cent lead oxide, is used to make drinking glasses.

Find out more about the group 4 elements

The table below contains some information about the properties of the **elements** in group 4.

Element	Symbol	Atomic number	Melting point (°C)	Boiling point (°C)	Density (g/cm³)
carbon	C	6	3527	4027	2.27 (graphite) 3.51 (diamond)
silicon	Si	14	1414	2900	2.33
germanium	Ge	32	938	2820	5.32
tin	Sn	50	232	2602	7.31
lead	Pb	82	327	1749	11.34

Compounds

These tables show you the chemical formulas of most of the **compounds** mentioned in the book. For example, carbon dioxide has the formula CO_2. This means it is made from one carbon **atom** and two oxygen atoms, joined together by chemical **bonds**. All the compounds are solids, except for the liquids, gases, acids and bases.

Oxides

Oxides	formula
aluminium oxide	Al_2O_3
calcium oxide	CaO
germanium oxide	GeO_2
iron oxide	Fe_2O_3
lead oxide	PbO
silicon dioxide	SiO_2
sodium oxide	Na_2O
tin oxide (cassiterite)	SnO_2

Carbonates

Carbonates	formula
calcium carbonate	$CaCO_3$
magnesium carbonate	$MgCO_3$
sodium carbonate	Na_2CO_3

Silicon compounds	formula
calcium silicate	$CaSiO_3$
magnesium silicate	$MgSiO_3$
silicon carbide	SiC
sodium silicate	Na_2SiO_3
zirconium silicate	$ZrSiO_4$
silicon dioxide	SiO_2

Silicon compounds

Germanium compounds	formula
argyrodite	Ag_8GeS_6
bismuth germanate	$Bi_4Ge_3O_{12}$
germanite	$Cu_{26}Fe_4Ge_4S_{32}$
germanium oxide	GeO_2
magnesium germanate	Mg_2GeO_4

Germanium compounds

Tin compounds	formula
tin chloride	$SnCl_2$
tin sulphate	$SnSO_4$
tributyl tin	$C_{12}H_{28}Sn$

Tin compounds

Lead compounds	formula
lead ethanoate	$(CH_3COO)_2Pb$
lead oxide	PbO
lead sulphate	$PbSO_4$
lead sulphide	PbS

Lead compounds

Acids	formula
carbonic acid	H_2CO_3
hydrochloric acid	HCl
sulphuric acid	H_2SO_4

Acids

Find out more continued

Bases

Bases	formula
limewater	$Ca(OH)_2$
sodium hydroxide	$NaOH$

Gases

Gases	formula
carbon dioxide	CO_2
carbon monoxide	CO
methane	CH_4
ethene	C_2H_4
propene	C_3H_6
hydrogen	H_2
oxygen	O_2

Liquids

Liquids	formula
ethanol	C_2H_5OH
silicon tetrachloride	$SiCl_4$
water	H_2O

Other compounds

Other compounds	formula
ammonium sulphate	$(NH_4)_2SO_4$
copper sulphate	$CuSO_4$
glucose	$C_6H_{12}O_6$

Glossary

alkenes hydrocarbons in which two or more carbon atoms are joined to each other by double bonds (two bonds, not just one)

allotropes two or more different forms of an element. Allotropes have the same chemical properties but different physical properties.

alloy mixture of two or more metals, or mixture of a metal and a non-metal. Alloys are often more useful than the pure metal on its own.

amorphous substance that does not contain any crystals

anodising making a layer of oxide on the surface of a metal using electrolysis

antioxidant substance that prevents oxygen reacting with other chemicals

atom the smallest particle of an element that has the property of that element. Atoms contain smaller particles called sub-atomic particles.

atomic number the number of protons in the nucleus of an atom. It is also called the proton number. No two elements have the same atomic number.

bond force that joins atoms together

brittle word that describes a solid that breaks into small pieces when hit. Glass is a brittle solid because it breaks into small pieces of glass when hit with a hammer.

bunny suit protective clothing that stops dust, skin and hair getting into a 'clean room'

carbohydrate compound that contains carbon, hydrogen and oxygen atoms. Sugars, starch and cellulose are carbohydrates.

catalyst substance that speeds up reactions without getting used up

ceramic tough solid made by heating clay and other substances to high temperatures in an oven. Plates, bathroom tiles and toilet bowls are made from ceramics.

combustion chemical reaction in which heat is produced, usually by a fuel reacting with oxygen in the air

compound substance made from the atoms of two or more elements, joined together by chemical bonds. Compounds can be broken down into simpler substances, and they have different properties from the elements in them. For example, water is a liquid at room temperature, but it is made from two gases, hydrogen and oxygen.

destructive distillation method used to produce new substances by heating solid or liquid carbon compounds to a very high temperature minus oxygen

distillation method used to separate a liquid from a mixture of a liquid and a solid. It works because the liquid has a lower boiling point than the solid.

electrolysis breaking down or decomposing a compound by passing electricity through it. The compound must be molten or dissolved in a liquid for electrolysis to work.

electrons subatomic particles with a negative electric charge. They are found in shells around the nucleus of an atom.

element substance made from one type of atom. Elements cannot be broken down into simpler substances. All substances are made from one or more elements.

enzyme catalyst made by living things. It is made from proteins, and controls the chemical reactions that happen in living things.

fermentation reaction caused by the enzymes in tiny fungi called yeast. In fermentation, sugar is broken down to make alcohol and carbon dioxide.

fertilizer chemical that gives plants the elements they need for healthy growth

fossil fuel fuel made from the ancient remains of dead animals or plants. It is a non-renewable fuel because once it runs out, it cannot be replaced. Coal, oil and natural gas are fossil fuels.

fractional distillation type of distillation that is used to separate mixtures of two or more liquids. It works because the liquids have different boiling points.

fungicide chemical that kills the fungus that can damage crops

groups vertical columns of elements in the periodic table. Elements in a group have similar properties.

hydrocarbon compound made from hydrogen and carbon atoms only

impermeable rock rock that does not let liquids and gases through it

insecticide chemical that kills insects that can damage crops

malleable the word that describes a solid that can be bent into shape without breaking. Metals and alloys are malleable.

mineral substance that is found naturally but does not come from animals or plants. Metal ores and limestone are examples of minerals.

neutralization reaction between an acid and an alkali or a base. The solution made is neutral, which means it is not acidic or alkaline.

neutron subatomic particle with no electric charge. It is found in the nucleus of an atom.

nucleus the part of an atom made from protons and neutrons. It has a positive electric charge and is found at the centre of the atom.

ore contains minerals from which metals can be taken out and purified

period horizontal row of elements in the periodic table

periodic table the table in which all the known elements are arranged into groups and periods

permeable rock rock that lets liquids and gases through it because it contains tiny holes and cracks

photolithography process of transferring shapes from a mask to the surface of a silicon wafer

photosynthesis chemical reaction that green plants use to make sugars from carbon dioxide and water using the energy from light. Oxygen is also made.

pigment solid substance that gives colour to a paint. A pigment does not dissolve in water.

polymer large molecule made from lots of smaller molecules joined together. Plastic is a polymer.

product the substance made in a chemical reaction

proton subatomic particle with a positive electric charge. It is found in the nucleus of an atom.

reaction chemical change that produces new substances

reduction taking away oxygen from an element or compound in a chemical reaction.

refining removing impurities from a substance to make it more pure. It can also mean separating the different substances in a mixture, for example, in oil refining.

semi-conductor a substance, such as silicon, that is an electrical insulator at room temperature, but a conductor when it is warmed or other elements are added to it

zone-refining a method used to make pure crystals by melting and freezing impure crystals

Timeline

carbon discovered	ancient times	unknown
tin discovered	ancient times	unknown
lead discovered	ancient times	unknown
diamonds are made of carbon	1772	Antoine Lavoisier
graphite is made of carbon	1779	Carl Scheele
silicon discovered	1823	Jöns Berzelius
germanium discovered	1886	Clemens Winkler
buckminsterfullerene, C_{60}, discovered	1985	Richard Smalley, Robert Curl and Harold Kroto
ununquadium first made	1998	Lawrence Berkeley National Laboratory, USA

Further reading and useful websites

Books

Fullick, Ann, *Science Topics: Chemicals in Action* (Heinemann Library, 1999)

Oxlade, Chris, *Chemicals in Action* series, particularly *Atoms; Elements and Compounds* (Heinemann Library, 2002)

Knapp, Brian, *The Elements* series, particularly, *Carbon; Silicon; Lead and Tin* (Atlantic Europe Publishing Co., 1996)

Websites

WebElements™
http://www.webelements.com
An interactive periodic table crammed with information and photographs.

DiscoverySchool
http://school.discovery.com/students
Help for science projects and homework, and free science clip art.

Proton Don
http://www.funbrain.com/periodic
The fun periodic table quiz!

BBC Science
http://www.bbc.co.uk/science
Quizzes, news, information and games about all areas of science.

Creative Chemistry
http://www.creative-chemistry.org.uk
An interactive chemistry site with fun practical activities, quizzes, puzzles and more.

Mineralogy Database
http://www.webmineral.com
Lots of useful information about minerals, including colour photographs and information about their chemistry.

Index

Titles in the *Periodic Table* series include:

Hardback   0 431 16981 0

Hardback   0 431 16982 9

Hardback   0 431 16984 5

Hardback   0 431 16983 7

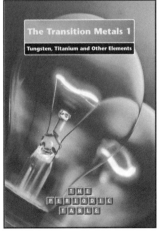

Hardback   0 431 16985 3

Hardback   0 431 16980 2

Find out about the other titles in this series on our website www.heinemann.co.uk/library